THE WOMA

E
WOMAN'S
GUIDE TO
AUTO
RACING

ARLENE MARTIN
JANET PRENSKY

AVERY PUBLISHING GROUP
Garden City Park • New York

Cover Designer: Doug Brooks
Typesetters: John and Rhonda Wincek
Original Interior Art: John Wincek
In-House Editor: Marie Caratozzolo

The following photos have been reprinted with permission:

- Mario Andretti (page 53). Photographer: Ken Osburn/ Index Stock Imagery.
- "King" Richard Petty (page 57). Photographer: Paul Butterbrodt/Index Stock Imagery.
- Mark Martin (on cover). Photographer: Steven Rose.
- Mark Martin's car (on cover). Photographer: Steven Rose.
- Mark, Arlene, and Matt Martin (page 81). Photographer: Steven Rose.

Avery Publishing Group
120 Old Broadway
Garden City Park, NY 11040
1–800–548–5757
www.averypublishing.com

Woman SportsFan™
www.sportsfan.com

ISBN 0-89529-991-7

Printed in the United States of America

10 9 8 7 6 5 4 3 2 1

Contents

About Woman SportsFan™

Once upon a time, the area of sports was dominated by men. Women rarely watched, participated in, or even dared ask questions about such activities. Today, thankfully, this has changed. For millions of women, sports are an important and integral part of their lives, which is why Woman SportsFan (WSF) was born. An outstanding resource for the increasing number of women everywhere who want to learn more about professional sports, Woman SportsFan presents a wealth of information specifically from a woman's perspective.

Log onto their website at WWW.SPORTSFAN.COM to discover a variety of sources from which you can glean sports information—and more than just stats! Here you can have questions answered by professional staff members, participate in games and contests, and experience special interactive WSF events. You can also enjoy the Woman SportsFan special book series. Written by women for women, this group of entertaining, fun, easy-to-read-and-understand books presents basic information on a number of professional sports. Each book is witty and entertaining, and, best of all, informative.

So whether you need information on auto racing, golf, football, or any other professional sport, turn to Woman SportsFan as your premier provider. Learn and enjoy!

Acknowledgments

This book was written with the help and support of many. Thanks go to Andy Miller, Donna LaVita-Tefft and all the great people at MarkeTVision for their fair feedback and gentle prodding. Thanks also to Kristine Indelicato, Dorien Rizzo, and Brian Sweeney for their overall contributions to this project, and to Dave Grossnickle, known in these parts as "Auto Racing Man," for his invaluable suggestions and enthusiasm in the production of this book. Sincere gratitude to Marie Caratozzolo, our editor at Avery Publishing, for her patience and sense of humor. Special thanks to Arnold Prensky for all of those driving lessons. And a special thank you to Anne-Marie Aigner who one day said, "Why don't you write a book on auto racing?" Good idea!

Foreword

They say you get out of life what you put into it. Well, I'm living proof of that. Although I'm not big on preaching or philosophizing, I do believe that auto racing is more than just a little bit like life in that it takes ambition, drive, and a lot of hard work to succeed. I know that there are a lot of people out there, mostly women, who don't understand the sport but do understand the importance of picking something you like and working hard at it. That's what I did with auto racing and I've never looked back. So, even if you don't understand why we like driving fast, getting dirty, and sometimes risking life and limb just to come in first, after reading this book, I hope you'll understand that we do it because we love it. And surely you understand what it's like to have a dream. I'm one of the lucky ones. I have gotten to live my dream. I race cars for a living, grew up with the greatest parents a guy could have, and spend my days with a phenomenal wife and kids. I have been blessed in so many ways.

When I first met my wife, Arlene, she could have cared less about auto racing. She thought, possibly like you, that driving around in a circle for hours was a pretty strange way to spend your time. But, she's grown to like the sport because she's learned more about it and understands some of the strategies and intricacies that make it up. (That and the fact that it's pretty tough to be married to a driver and be allergic to racing!) I hope this book will help you like the sport more because you'll get to know it better, too. You may be surprised to find out how many women love auto racing and come to all the races. It's really an exciting sport, and it offers something to everyone—kids, men, women, passionate fans, and brand new ones.

I got involved in racing with the support of my dad. He was my hero and I think he always will be. My dad was the type of guy who didn't have many, if any, regrets. He lived his life to the fullest, and he believed in working hard, playing hard, and trying hard. He used to say, "Maybe other people are satisfied to remain where they are and be king of the hill there. Everytime we became king of the hill we headed up to a higher hill." That's the kind of guy my dad was, and every opportunity I have to tell people about him I do because I'm so proud of him and so thankful to him for everything he did for me.

But along with hard work, my dad believed in having fun, and so do I. And so should you! So read through this book, learn a little something about auto racing, and have a lotta fun. And maybe by the end, you'll understand why we love driving fast in circles so much! It may seem monotonous, but believe me, if you joined me for a day of racing, you would be anything but bored!

Mark Martin is one of the greatest drivers in NASCAR history. In 1997, he became the "winningest" driver in NASCAR Busch Series history with thirty-two wins. The senior driver on the Roush Racing Team, Martin is one of only seven racers in the modern era to record four victories in a row.

Why This Book?

This book is the answer for women everywhere who find themselves clueless about auto racing. And that's a lot of women, so don't feel alone!

Maybe you've found yourself sitting in a room and everyone around you is talking about very fast cars. You drive a Honda, and on a daring day you push it to 65. You add this to the conversation. Everyone looks at you funny. This book is for you.

Maybe you have a husband or boyfriend who spends his time in front of the TV watching cars go round and round a track. He turns to you and says, "Can you believe it?" You don't know whether it's right to say, "Yes, I can believe it. Thank heavens." Or "No, I can't believe it. What a shock." This book is for you.

Maybe, like some of us, you're married to top race-car driver Mark Martin. Okay, so this book isn't for you. But there better be only one of us, or someone's sleeping on the couch tonight!

This book is for those of you who just want to know what all the hubbub is about. You're aware that auto racing is hot, and you want to know why. Let this book be your guide.

You will learn the basics of auto racing. Not too much. Just enough to function in this strange land. It will be like learning enough French to survive in Paris for a week's vacation. You'll learn how to say, "Where's the bathroom?" but you won't learn how to say, "Is the design of this bathroom influenced by Greek or Roman architecture?" You don't need to know that much. And this book will not go that far. It will go just far enough to give you the tools to add a little something to the conversation or to at least understand four of every ten words spoken on the sport. Who needs to go ten-for-ten? That's unheard of in sports anyway!

Sports can be intimidating, but they can also be pretty interesting, so sit back and let this book take you to a new world. You may shock yourself and even enjoy it.

Imagine the look on your friends' faces when you're as versed on the Indy 500 as you are on Beverly Hills 90210. And when you know that although "The King" may be Elvis, King Richard is auto racing's Richard Petty. And that you can just as easily watch ESPN as you can MTV or the WB.

You'll be smarter than you were when you started. But not too smart. After all, no one likes a smartie pants. Not to worry. This book will make you a kinda, sorta smartie pants. Nothing wrong with that!

Gentlewomen . . . start your engines!

1 What Is Auto Racing?

The premise of auto racing is the simplest of all sports. First one to finish wins. This, as you know, is not true for everything. Many of us have often finished our midterm exams first, but that was because we knew so little we had nothing to write. Or how about finishing first at the dinner table? Fast eating is not considered a victory, it's considered gluttony, and get the spinach out of your teeth.

But auto racing is about going the fastest and finishing first. Pure and simple. Sounds easy, but of course it's not. The distance between the start and the finish varies from race to race, and along the way terrible things can happen. A driver's car can hit a wall. A driver's car can hit another car. A driver's car can hit an oil slick and spin out of control. A driver's car can run out of gas and come to a complete, humiliating stop. A driver's car can have one of a variety of mechanical problems, forcing it out of the race. (You may not be shocked to discover that when a transmission falls out

Auto Racing in Ten Words or Less

Man in car. Goes fast. Turns left. Wins.

Auto Racing Loss in Ten Words or Less

Man in car. Goes fast. Turns right. Crashes into wall.

Auto Racing Broadcast in Ten Words or Less

Here they come again.
Here they come again.

of a car, for example, it will impact that vehicle's success.) A driver can have one of a variety of mental problems resulting in a car losing a race. (Please see sentence above about the car running out of gas.) Stuff happens, as they say, and auto racing is no exception. So going fast and coming in first can be a simple concept riddled with complex problems.

A race car driver also doesn't have it as easy as it seems. Looks simple. Sit in a car, push on the accelerator pedal to go fast, step on the brake to slow down and stop. We've all done it. What's the big deal? The big deal is this is not bumper-to-bumper rush-hour traffic on a highway near your home. This is 200-mile-per-hour racing! All right. Many of us, and I won't name names, have gone over the speed limit. We've done 70 in a 55 mile-an-hour zone.

We've done 80. Many have even done 90 with that middle finger raised in triumph as we pass that slowpoke who's been driving 45 in the left lane for the last two miles. But we don't know from 200 miles per hour. We don't know the conditioning required for driving at that speed. Or the reflexes. Or the courage. Auto racing is a sport and the drivers are athletes. And, of course, those athletes are millionaires. But more on that later.

So let's take it slowly and get to know the various components that make up this popular sport. We'll meet the cars, the tracks, and the drivers. We'll get to know some of the terms of auto racing and some of the great races that have taken place over the years. We'll learn about the money involved in the sport, the top moneymakers, and the movers and the shakers. We'll learn how it all started and where it seems to be going. And then we'll stop. Not because we've run out of gas, just out of words. This is a guide, not an encyclopedia. And for that, we are all extremely grateful.

2 In the Beginning . . . Man Created a Very Slow Car

It's not easy to pinpoint the exact moment that we moved from a horse-and-buggy world to a motorized one—from "Has anybody seen my whip?" to "Has anybody seen my keys?" But, the late 1800s seem to receive the greatest consensus. German Nicholas Otto developed an internal combustion engine in 1878. German Karl Benz added a motor to a tricycle in 1885, and, although inevitably looking like a fool putt-putting around on his kid's bike, that trike did move. German engineer (why were those Germans in such a hurry?) Gottlieb Daimler, in that same year, perfected Otto's internal combustion engine and was able to move a four-wheeled gasoline-powered carriage. Things were really hopping then, and an automobile boom took place between 1895 and 1908 in France. The Germans may have held the edge in inventiveness, but France held the edge in roads. They had them, for example, and that was quite an edge. And the roads in France were said to be superior to all others, oui?

Obviously, a road without a car is no fun, so France kicked into high gear and dominated this early era in terms of automobile design and production. But what about us, you ask? What were the Americans doing? Why, dreaming up the Edsel, silly. Actually, we were working, too. On September 21, 1893, Charles and Frank Duryea of Springfield, Massachusetts, developed the country's first car powered by an internal combustion engine. It was only a one-cylinder engine, but the Duryeas were giddy just the same.

In 1899, Ransom Olds opened the Olds Motor Works in Detroit, where he produced the first car to be made in large numbers—the Oldsmobile. That baby moved at a blurring 14 miles per hour. Then came a guy you've probably heard of—Henry Ford. In

Who Knew?

The first American auto race took place in 1895 in Chicago, Illinois. It was a fifty-four-mile race won by J. Frank Duryea in a Duryea car. Frank's average speed was a blurring 7.5 miles an hour. Rumor has it that Frank is currently driving the streets of Boca Raton, Florida. Don't you recall being behind him the last time you visited your grandparents?

1908, the Ford Motor Company perfected the mass production of cars, and people started buying them. In that year, approximately 65,000 cars were sold, most of them Ford's Model T. But people being people, they weren't happy. Are we ever? Cars broke down, they were noisy, they were smelly. Carmakers needed to deal with public perception that their creations were, how shall we say, not perfect. One ad for Ford's Model A was this charmer, "It is positively the most perfect machine on the market, having overcome all drawbacks such as smell, noise, jolt, etc., common to all other makes of auto carriages." Yummy. I'll take two!

Automakers had to do something to win back the public. Something bigger than life. And . . . ta da . . . auto racing in America was born!

Although the first American automobile race is said to have taken place in 1895 in Chicago and won by Frank Duryea traveling a blistering 7.5 miles per hour, it was Henry Ford who built the first real American race car, which he named the "999." His test driver, Barney Oldfield, became the first person to drive 60 miles per hour. Talk about really moving!

It was in 1908, though, that the greatest race ever took place. It was the New York to Paris race and it began in Times Square with six teams of drivers and their six cars. The cars were a who's who in international automotive circles with one American Thomas Flyer car, one Italian Zust car, one German Protos car, and three French cars—a Moto-Bloc, a Sizaire-Naudin, and a De Dion (no relation to Celine). Vrroom, cough, cough, Vrrooom, cough, cough . . . they were off! The contestants sputtered up Broadway out of Times Square dreaming of croissants and café au lait. The first leg of the race had them crossing the United States to San Francisco. There they were shipped first to Seattle and then to Alaska, where they drove to Nome. From Nome they were shipped across the Pacific Ocean. After the crossing, they had to drive through Siberia, on to Moscow, down to Berlin, and then, mon dieu, to Paris. At least, that was the plan.

The French Sizaire-Naudin bid the race adieu in upstate New York. The French Moto-Bloc got stuck on the slushy roads of Iowa and had to say au revoir. The German Protos came to a halt in Idaho but would not give up. The car was moved by train to Seattle, where it was repaired. Next, it was loaded onto a freighter and ferried over to Siberia. The never-say-die Americans also went a roundabout way. They made it to Alaska, but the roads were impossible so they sailed for Japan. Wouldn't you? After a little sushi and I daresay a lot of sake, they too, then shipped their car to Siberia.

By now, our auto racers had been traveling for ninety-nine days! Paris was a mere 8,000 miles away. While many of us would now be weeping, our fearless adventurers plowed ahead. Well, some of them anyway. The De Dion car withdrew, leaving no French entries heading home to Paris. The Italian Zust could not keep up and fell way, way behind. So it was all left to the German Protos and the American Thomas Flyer. And off they went, fender to fender, for two months across Asia, through Europe . . . sniffing the air for a whiff of coq au vin. But the Americans met

And You Should Have Seen the Other Car . . .

This is a classic. On January 16, 1952, the Florida Stock Car Championships were in full gear with two cars in a fender-to-fender fight to the finish. Rags Carter had the lead, but Edwin Matthews would have none of that. He drew even and pushed Rags to the rail. Rags' wheels got caught on the wall and his whole front axle was torn off. What was left of his car, with Rags still inside, then flipped over and landed on its top facing backward. Before anyone knew what was happening, the car skidded across the finish line upside down and backwards, and beat Matthews by a matter of seconds! Like the saying goes . . . "it ain't over, till it's over."

disaster near Moscow when their trusty Thomas Flyer broke down. Search as they did for a Thomas Flyer repair shop in Moscow, believe it or not, they couldn't find one, so they had to use Yankee ingenuity to somehow get that car back on its feet . . . tires. On July 30, 1908, exactly 167 days after the start of the race, the German Protos crossed the finish line in Paris. Four days later, the Thomas Flyer limped in. But the gods were smiling on those tired Americans. The German team was penalized fifteen days for their illegal train ride from Idaho to Seattle, so the Americans were declared the winners.

It should not surprise you to learn that this was the first and *only* race from New York to Paris. Not that it wasn't a good time . . .

3 So Many Cars . . .

Next to horse racing, auto racing is considered the most popular sport in the world. "World" is emphasized here, because auto racing is very international. In fact, as popular as it is in the United States, it may be even more so in Europe. To give you an idea of what we're talking about . . . a crowd at a baseball game may hover anywhere from 30,000 to 70,000 people, depending on the size of the ballpark. The Indy 500 has drawn as many as 300,000 people! That's just one race! When the Rolling Stones go on tour, they'd have to play six concerts to draw that many fans. And they sing different songs. There are some people who believe there has been only one Indy 500, and it is just replayed year after year. Kind of the Christmas fruitcake of sports! But we digress . . .

Just as there are different types of music from rock to rap to alternative to pop, there are different types of auto racing. In music, each type is distinct, has its own fans, its own stars, and its own style. But taken as a whole, all the types together make up the vast world of music. It's the same with auto racing. Many styles, many celebrities, many passionate followers. But, all together, it's just auto racing. And, just as Madonna goes on tour to earn money, so do auto racers. Their tours are called *circuits*, but besides the difference in terminology, the concept is the same. She hits the road and sings for the money. He hits the road and drives for the money. And we, of course, pay, pay, pay.

The rap, reggae, rock and roll, rhythm and blues, and pop of auto racing are stock car, Indy car, Formula One, sports car, and drag racing. What's the difference, you ask? Isn't it good you bought this little book? Here we go with some brief descriptions.

Stock Car Racing

Stock cars are the ones that look like regular cars (like that Ford in your neighbor's driveway) but go really fast—somewhere in the 200 mile-an-hour area. Stock cars are made of steel and weigh almost two tons . . . 3,700 pounds to be exact. So much for the common perception that big things can't go fast (my Uncle Moe notwithstanding—that guy could really move, especially when called to dinner!). Stock cars race, as a rule, on *superspeedways*. A superspeedway is a speedway with wide, high-banked turns. Why they just don't call it a wide, high-banked speedway is beyond me. All kidding aside, a superspeedway is where the "big-time" races like the Daytona 500 and the Indy 500 are held. They are at least one mile long and are the sites of the longer races—the ones that are hundreds of miles—for bigger money.

Legend has it that stock car racing began when bootleggers souped up their engines to escape the law. They took an old humble-looking Chevy, gave it lots of horsepower, and left the befuddled cops in the dust as they roared off into the sunset. This legend may have some truth to it as bootlegging had its origins in the South, and stock car racing began in the South with its popularity today still most pronounced in the South. So, we'll go with this legend, and so may you.

Stock car racing began as an organized sport in 1947. A group of stock car officials met in Daytona Beach, Florida, and formed the National Association for Stock Car Auto Racing, which is more commonly known as NASCAR. Bill France, who was a stock car racer, was the president of NASCAR from its inception through 1972.

One of the most famous NASCAR superspeedways is the Daytona International Speedway, which

Stock car

opened for business in 1959. The 2.5-mile track is home to the Daytona 500—a 500-mile race (am I moving too quickly for you?). This means (okay, pull out the calculator. 500 divided by 2.5 equals . . .) the race is 200 laps. Our friend Mark Martin won the Daytona 500 in 1993, traveling an average of 137.93 miles an hour, which means it took him under four hours to complete the race. Traveling a total distance of 500 miles on New York's Long Island Expressway during rush hour would take Mark just under four weeks.

NASCAR drivers can get very rich by going very fast. The most popular and most profitable racing circuit is the Winston Cup Series. In 1971, the R.J. Reynolds Tobacco Company took its Winston cigarette product and began to sponsor NASCAR. The Winston Cup Series consists of thirty-one races. The driver with the most points in this series gets $1.25 million. And there are bonuses, to boot! For instance, any driver who wins three of NASCAR's top four races in the same season wins $1 million. The top four races include the Daytona 500 (the largest prize money), the Winston 500 (the fastest average speeds), the Coca-Cola 600 (the longest race at 600 miles), and the Southern 500 (the oldest race—it began in 1950). No driver has ever won all four races, and only four drivers in history have won the bonus by winning three of the four. They are LeeRoy Yarborough in 1969, David Pearson in 1976, Bill Elliott in 1985, and Jeff Gordon in 1998. To give you an idea of the kind of money that can be made, in 1997, Gordon earned $6,375,658 in Winston Cup prize money. That will buy a lot of fuzzy dice for the rearview mirror!

By the way, NASCAR drivers are not big. For example, Mark Martin is 5 feet 6 inches tall and weighs 135 pounds. Jeff Gordon is 5 feet 7 inches tall and weighs 150 pounds. What is this? The auto racing diet? Ladies . . . forget Atkins, forget The Zone, forget Pritikin . . . it's the NASCAR diet! Eat all you want, then sit in a car for like 500 miles going 200 miles per hour. This is a regimen that could catch on! It certainly beats calorie-counting and jumping jacks.

Formula One Racing

You know Formula One cars. They're the ones with the big wheels, the thin pointed body, and the little cockpit that the driver sits in. They're the real "race car looking" race cars. A Formula One car is very similar to an airplane in design. Its body, called the *fuselage*, is made of carbon fiber. It is the most expensive racing car to build, which is very confusing as it has no fenders, only one seat, and doesn't even have a roof. I guess heated seats, a CD player, and passenger side air bags are out of the question. But I would still insist upon them.

For years, cars made by Ferrari, Mercedes Benz, and Alfa Romeo dominated Formula One racing. In the 1960s, Ford got into the act, as did Porsche, Honda, and Renault. Eventually, everyone joined in, including the Chevy Corvette, Jaguar, and Maserati. They had to build the car to conform to a "formula," which is a scientific-sounding configuration limiting engine size, number of horsepower, etc. I won't bore

Formula One

you with it. No one you know will be aware of it, why should you?

Formula One or "F-1," as it is known to those in the know, is the most popular form of auto racing in the world, of which the Grand Prix races are the most famous. Grand Prix is French for "large prize," which to me would be just completing one of these races alive, but to the pros it means, of course, hundreds of thousands of dollars.

The first Grand Prix race took place in 1906 in Lemans, France. Famous Grand Prix racers include Mario Andretti (as in "Slow down, George. Who do you think you are? Mario Andretti?"), Juan Fangio of Argentina, Jackie Stewart of Scotland, and Alain Prost of France, who retired in 1993 as the most successful driver in Grand Prix history. Prost won fifty-one times in his thirteen-year career.

In every country but the United States, Formula One is the most popular form of auto racing. It is arguably more challenging than the American style of racing, as Grand Prix courses often wind through city streets and narrow country roads, as opposed to our oval tracks that just go round and round ad infinitum. Formula One racers are constantly shifting gears, coping with bumpy ground or uneven pavement, and negotiating difficult, at times unexpected, curves and turns. Cars travel at speeds of more that 200 miles per hour on the straightaways but are forced to slow down to speeds as low as 30 miles per hour on some of those tricky turns.

Formula One racing is dominated by international drivers, not Americans. There is less money to be made, so less Americans compete. You know how we love our money. For many in all sports, unfortunately, money is *the* motivating factor. Auto racing is not exempt from this disease.

There are Grand Prix races in Australia, Argentina, Germany, Hungary, Italy, Spain, France, Monaco, even Luxembourg. You know how the Tour de France bicycle race winds through the streets with fans lining the sides? (You don't? Next for you . . . Every Woman's Guide to Bicycle Racing!) How about the Boston Marathon? Runners up and down hills, around bends, over the river and through the woods to grandmother's house they go? This is the style of Grand Prix racing. Right there on the streets with the people cheering on the sidelines.

Indy Car Racing

Indy car designers must have been dating Formula One designers because these cars, too, have plenty of nothing. No roof, no fenders, and just one seat. While stock cars weigh 3,700 pounds, Indy Cars have been on the Richard Simmons Deal-a-Meal plan and are a svelte 1,550 pounds. Indy cars go really fast. How about 240 miles per hour? How about 0 to 100 in 4.2 seconds? It takes most of us 4.2 seconds just to open our eyes in the morning!

Indy cars race on the following types of tracks—*superspeedways* (remember? they're the ones that are at least one mile long), *temporary road courses* (built on closed-off streets in big cities), and *permanent road courses* (the ones that run naturally in the countryside).

For decades, the United States Auto Club ran all Indy car races. In the late 1970s, the Championship Auto Racing Team (CART) was formed and took over. This organization's series is aptly called the CART Championship Series. Then in the mid 1990s, a feud among those in the CART organization resulted in a split and the formation of a new league called the Indy Racing League (IRL). The IRL named their series the IndyCar Series. Are you confused yet? Do they seriously expect us to understand all of this? (More on this feud in Chapter 5.)

Indy car

The Indianapolis 500 is the most famous Indy car race and the most famous auto race in the world. Sadly, it has been victimized by the feuding in the auto racing industry and has lost a number of famous drivers, as well as thousands of spectators and TV viewers. When the Indy 500 race became part of the newly formed IRL, CART was truly peeved. This prompted CART to create its own race, which takes place on Memorial Day weekend—the same weekend as the Indy 500. Welcome to auto racing! What a warm and fuzzy sport!

But, be that as it may, the actual cars are still called Indy cars. Not IndyCar, the series, but Indy car, the car. There will be a test on this at the end of the book. I, too, will fail it.

The first CART racing series took place in 1979 and included thirteen races. Today, the Indy Racing League and CART League together have over thirty races. Beside the Indy 500, other races in the IndyCar series include the Indy 200, the Charlotte 500, the Pep Boys 400K, the Phoenix 200, and the Lone Star 500K (the K stands for kilometers, in case you're not woozy enough at this point). The CART Championship Series has sixteen races, including the Budweiser 500 and the Motorola 300.

All Indy car racers accumulate points based on the order in which they finish a race. Top drivers in the IRL include Scott Goodyear and Eddie Cheever. In the CART organization, some of the big names are Michael Andretti and Paul Tracy.

This ends our discussion of Indy car racing; hopefully, for all time.

No Cheap Thrill

Guess what a brand new Indy car would run you. How about $420,000! And if you're the kind of driver who wants an engine in that car, you'll have to add another $40,000 to $140,000. And, if you expect that engine to last close to 100,000 miles (or as I might think . . . 100,000 years) you'd better sit down. That engine needs to be rebuilt every 500 miles! Cost of the rebuild is in the area of $25,000. Good lord. And, oh yeah . . . you want tires? Oh sure, it's never enough for you, is it? A set of tires runs about $1,200. How long do they last? Um . . . would you believe minutes? The pit crew changes those tires seven times during an average race. That's $8,400 in tires every race, not to mention a rebuilt $25,000 engine following every 500-mile event. Oh, and let's not forget that you'll need gas, and you'll also need to transport the car from race to race (you rarely see Indy cars on the highway heading from Indianapolis with a "Daytona or Bust" sign on the back bumper). All told, the estimated cost to race an Indy car is somewhere in the vicinity of $2.5 million. And that doesn't take into consideration the fuzzy dice!

Sports Car Racing

And you thought they were all sports cars, didn't you? See what you're learning? The Sports Car Club of America (SCCA) sponsors 2,000 amateur and professional races every year. The amateur racing circuit is called Club Racing, and this is where drivers can obtain their professional driving licenses. The SCCA sponsors about 250 of these amateur club races a year.

The top cars that compete in Sports Car racing are the Chevrolet Camaro, Ford Mustang, and Pontiac Trans Am. The sports car engine is just a plain old engine—it's not souped up. It's the same one you'll find in your own little Ford Mustang. The drivers just push it to the max and get it up to 200 miles an hour. This shows you what your world would be like without traffic. Imagine a 200-mile drive to work that took an hour. You could work in New York, live in Pennsylvania, and go home every day for lunch! Okay, so it's a bit of an exaggeration, but you get the idea.

The most famous pro racing sports car event is the Trans-Am Championship, which consists of fourteen races, each about 100 miles long (except for the endurance races discussed next) and total prize money of approximately $1.5 million. Total! Chicken feed in the world of auto racing, but better than the total prize money you and I have ever been offered for doing anything!

The sports car world also includes the unique *endurance races.* As opposed to the 400-, 500-, or 600-mile races that take a couple of hours, the winner of

Sports car

endurance racing is the team that goes the farthest in twenty-four hours. This can be as much as 2,500 miles! Emphasis here is on the word "team," as no one person could safely handle the skilled driving necessary over that amount of time. Three to five drivers normally comprise a team and act kind of like a relay team in track and field.

The two most famous endurance races are aptly called the 24 Hours of LeMans and the 24 Hours of Daytona. Most consider the 24 Hours of LeMans, which takes place over 8.5 miles in LeMans, France, the most important of all international road races. What Indy is to track races, LeMans is to road races. This is a very tough race, run on the public roads of LeMans complete with challenging terrain, twists, and turns. The car is king in this race and it is actually the car itself that is named the winner. Porsche, Peugeot, Ferrari, Ford, and Jaguar have won the prize numerous times over the history of the race, which began in 1923. The 24 Hours of LeMans usually covers 1,000 miles, which indicates the difficulty of the race.

The 24 Hours of Daytona, on the other hand, can cover 2,500 miles, as it is held at the Daytona International Speedway—a much less-challenging course that is much more predictable and easier to manage. Each 3.56-mile lap includes Daytona's oval track as well as its adjoining road course, which is situated in the track's interior area. Believe it or not, in 1996, after 24 hours, 697 laps, and 2,481.32 miles, the Oldsmobile team beat the Ferrari team by only 65 seconds! The 24 Hours at Daytona is the opening event of the International Motor Sports Association (IMSA—what's a paragraph without an acronym?) sports car season, which includes the nine-race Exxon World Sports Car Championship.

The Fastest Cars in the World

The fastest cars in the world are called land-speed racers. They look a lot like missiles and could be mistaken for them because they go almost as fast! In 1983, a British racer named Richard Noble clocked in with the world's fastest land-speed record of 633.468 miles per hour! This is not a typo! Ever since, at the Bonneville Salt Flats in Utah, drivers have attempted to top this amazing record. At the time of this writing, Noble's record remains intact.

Drag Racing

You're waiting at a stoplight and some young whippersnapper drives up next to you and revs his engine . . . Vrooom, vrooom. The light turns green and off he goes, leaving you to eat his dust. This, my friend, was a drag race, and you did not win! As they say . . . don't quit the day job.

Drag racing is a mano-a-mano or auto-a-auto sport. Two cars race from a standing start over a drag strip, which is a straight paved track of a quarter mile in length. Fastest car wins. And, in some cases that fastest car can go 300 miles per hour and cover that quarter mile in 4.5 seconds!

There are three types of cars in drag racing—Top Fuel (also known as dragsters), Funny Car, and Pro Stock. Top Fuel is the fastest. In fact, Top Fuel cars, which run on super-high-power nitro-methane fuel, can accelerate faster than any other fast-moving machine, including the Concorde. We're talking 0 to 100 miles per hour in less than 1 second. These scary,

Top Fuel Dragster

Funny Car

fast-moving things have 6,000-horsepower engines (your Hyundai chugs along with about 150 horses powering it). Top Fuel cars, which look a bit like long cigars, have small spoked front tires and large 17-inch-wide rear tires. These cars move so fast, when they start, their front wheels lift from the ground and stay up in the air for the first 100 feet of the race. At the end of the race, the driver releases two parachutes that serve as brakes. Together, car and driver must weigh at least 1,975 pounds . . . hopefully the car covering most of that!

A Funny Car looks like an ordinary Dodge or Chevy passenger car, but that's where the similarity ends. This car is like a wolf in sheep's clothing—its innocent-looking carbon fiber body contains the same powerful engine as a Top Fuel car. And like their Top Fuel cousins, Funny Cars run on nitro methane and need parachutes to decelerate at the end of each race. Their minimum weight, including the driver, is 2,225 pounds.

Pro Stock cars are post-1989 two-door passenger sedans with household names like Ford, Chevy, and Dodge. Unlike the 6,000-horsepower engines of the

Pro Stock Car

Top Fuel and Funny Cars, the Pro Stock car engines rev at only 1,200 or 1,300 horsepower. I say, only, but in reality this is eight times more powerful than the average car.

The National Hot Rod Association (NHRA) oversees drag racing and has nearly 85,000 members and 30,000 licensed drivers. It is the largest motorsports organization in the world. Comparatively, the Sports Car Club of America has 50,000 members.

Approximately 2 million people attend drag meets every year. A drag meet includes elimination rounds. It's driver versus driver with the winner advancing to meet the next driver, and so on and so on. The one left standing is the champion.

There you have it. The many types of cars and races that make up the mad, mad, mad, mad world of auto racing. Each type of race has its own fans and its own distinct style, but all are united by the same goal that drives all sports—victory. And in auto racing, victory goes to the fastest. And to the fastest goes the big pot of gold at the end of the speedway. And that brings us to our next chapter and the answer to that age-old question . . . if you drive on a speedway, why in heaven's name can't you speed in a driveway?

SPONSORED BY SPARK PLUGS, BEER NUTS, AND LUBE

One glance at the names of the sponsors in auto racing and there is no doubt who their target audience is. MEN! Men with trucks! Men who drink beer! Men who like to get smelly stuff on their hands after hours in the garage. Look at the companies that sponsor races—Craftsman Trucks, Valvoline, Marlboro, Miller Lite, Jiffy Lube, Dura Lube (where the heck do you put all that lube, you guys? And what is lube anyway?), AC Delco, Goodwrench, Budweiser, batteries, tools, tires . . . there's even a Bosch Spark Plug Grand Prix. Good lord . . . booze, butts, and batteries, both car and household. Guy things. The targeted guys are predominately those from the heartland, who were brought up driving trucks and watching auto racing. Stereotype? Probably, but I firmly believe this is more truth than fiction. Despite what those folks from the left and right coast may think, these guys who love auto racing must spend a lot of money. Corporate America wants them and wants them badly.

Let's think about this. Sponsorship is a very savvy marketing tool. Take the Virginia Slims Tennis Tournament. This "female" cigarette sponsors women's tennis. Makes sense despite the fact that cigarettes and running back and forth on a tennis court do not mix. The decision to sponsor a sporting event is never taken lightly. These are million-dollar decisions that can have million-dollar returns.

In auto racing, large corporations began seeing the light in the 1960s, when company logos started sprouting up on race cars everywhere. Winning a big race translated into big dollars. Not only did racing pit driver against driver, it also became a battle of big business.

Auto racing is one of the most heavily and shamelessly sponsored sporting events that exist. Everything associated with the sport has a corporate sponsor. From the overall series, such as the Winston Cup, to the races themselves, like the Lysol 200 (a personal favorite—whodathunkit?), to the cars that are slapped with logos for everything from soft drinks to gasoline, to the drivers' clothes, hats, you name it. I wouldn't be surprised if some of their pets are branded with an Alpo logo.

And this stuff isn't cheap either. Primary sponsorship in the Winston Cup series, which is the creme de la creme of stock car racing, is $5 to $8 million! To compete in the lower level Grand National circuit, you'd need from $2 to $3 million in sponsorships. When you look at numbers like these, you realize that maybe something's going on in the world that deserves our attention. Auto racing is a multi-multi-million dollar business. We can poo poo it all we want and consider it just some guys driving really fast, but the following fact cannot be denied. Between the sponsorships and the TV contracts, auto racing is a huge business. Of course, all sports are considered huge business, but auto racing may be the biggest of them all.

Although it cannot be argued that male-oriented sponsors pervade racing, there are a number of advertisers who recognize that women exist, too, and some of us are even watching. Hanes and Tide are auto racing sponsors, and if you look closely, you'll see a Betty Crocker car in the Daytona 500. But just imagine if auto racing sponsors took the female gender into serious consideration. Just where are those sponsored races for women?

- Forget NASCAR's Diehard 500. Where is our Lady-Di Hard 500?
- The Bud 400? Where's our Dry Martini With a Twist 400?
- STP Oil sponsored cars? Would an FTD Florist sponsored car hurt?
- Wouldn't we be more apt to watch a race sponsored by Jiffy Pop than Jiffy Lube?

Because this sport's actual corporate sponsors are so male-oriented, one may feel that auto racing truly is just for men and not something women really need to know about. Allow me to reiterate this book's overall theme—a little knowledge on a lot of subjects is a good thing. If there's something out there that major corporations are sinking millions and millions of dollars into, shouldn't we at least know something about it? We don't need to speak fluent auto racing, but certainly we should know how to say, "Where is the ladies room?" in auto-ese. This is our goal.

So, now that we know a little about auto racing dough-re-mi, we can ask only, "What about us?" Think about it corporate America.

4 The Tracks of Their Cheers

There are many kinds of tracks in auto racing. Again, in music, you have CDs, cassettes, and that old chestnut, the record album. In auto racing, you have oval tracks, winding tracks, big tracks, small tracks, dirt tracks, clay tracks, and paved tracks. There are hundreds and hundreds of tracks throughout the world, ranging from small quarter-mile tracks to tracks that are over twelve miles around. Pike's Peak Hill Climb in Colorado Springs, for instance, has a twelve-and-a-half-mile lap. Unlike professional football fields, basketball courts, and baseball diamonds, which are all regulation sized, race tracks march to the tune of a different drummer. (See examples of various track lengths and shapes on pages 38 and 39.) So many tracks, so little time. Let's take a look at a few of them.

Indianapolis Motor Speedway

The Indianapolis Motor Speedway, where the famous Indy 500 is run, is a two-and-a-half mile oval track. Bill Vukovich, a driver who won the Indy 500 twice in the 1950s said of this track, "Just remember one thing. Always turn left." Basically that's the key for those ovals. That and holding on for dear life, as turning left when you're going 200 miles per hour can't be easy.

Information about the Indianapolis Motor Speedway can fill a book, but for the sake of brevity, we'll keep it to a paragraph. First of all, it's huge. How many speedways can house a museum and an 18-hole championship-caliber golf course within the track's infield area? Give up? None but Indy. Its Speedway Museum has, as you might guess, lots of racing memorabilia, cool cars, and racing movies to enjoy. Its golf course, which includes 72 sand traps, 650 trees, and 3 lakes, is the site of the Senior PGA Tour's Brickyard Crossing Championship. Trackside gift shops are everywhere. It's a bit like Disney World with more souvenir T-shirts and bumper stickers and refrigerator magnets than you can imagine. And, of course, there are parties everywhere at the Speedway during Indy 500 week, particularly tent parties with plenty of drinks, lots of food, and loud music. Just another Saturday night in the dorm.

Daytona International Speedway

The Daytona International Speedway in Florida, where the famous Daytona 500 occurs, is a superspeedway

THE BIG KAHUNA—THE INDY 500

"I felt I had been sucked into a hundred-mile-an-hour tornado. I was never so scared in my life."

—American racer Wilbur Shaw
After experiencing his first race at Indianapolis in 1924

Since the goal of this book is to arm you with just a couple of good nuggets to pass around at the next beer blast you attend with truckers and mechanics, let's learn in-depth about one race and only one race. The one you've heard of, the one everybody's heard of, the one even I have heard of—the Indy 500.

Held each year on Memorial Day weekend, the Indianapolis 500 began in 1911. The 2.5-mile track is called "The Brickyard" because it was paved initially with 3 million bricks. It has since been paved over but still has a ceremonial strip of bricks at the starting line.

The Indy 500 is considered by racecar drivers to be the ultimate—the race above all others that they most want to win. To some, the Indy 500 is more than a race. It's become a religion. Driver Eddie Sachs once said, "I think of Indianapolis every day of the year, every hour of the day, and when I sleep, too. On the morning of the race, if you told me my house had burned down, I'd say, 'So what?'" Eddie's house did not burn down, but his car did. During the 1964 Indy 500, Eddie's car went up in flames and he was killed.

At times, there have been over 300,000 people in the stands at the Indy 500. Compare that to Fenway Park's 30,000 and we are talking lots of spectators. There are close to 220,000 permanent seats at Indy, and another 15,000 seats can be installed overnight. Typically, more than 30,000 people stand in the infield during the race. Add it all up, and you have almost three times as many people as those that attend the Kentucky Derby and the most densely populated 500-acre area in the entire world. Whew!

The first person to win the Indy 500 was Ray Harroun, driving at an average speed of just over 74 miles per hour. Harroun is also responsible for an automobile feature that most of us take for granted. He had the great idea that, although he was driving forward, it might be helpful to see who was behind him. Thus, the rearview mirror was born. Way to go, Ray! Thanks to you, all of us now know just how pissed the person behind us is after we cut them off in the high-speed lane!

Speeds at the Indy 500 were clocked in the 100s in the 1920s, the 120s in the 1930s, and onward and upward in the years that followed. In 1990, Arie Luyendyk won the race with a speed of 185.981 miles per hour, still an Indy record.

> One of the greatest Indy 500s of all time took place in 1992. This was not a pretty Indy. Of the thirty-three cars starting the race, twelve finished. After 190 of the total 200 laps, Al Unser, Jr. and Scott Goodyear were fender to fender. Scott, a bit behind, kept trying to pass; but Al, Jr., the little devil, kept swerving back and forth to prevent him. This, I might add, while going 220 miles per hour! With just 300 feet left, Scott rushed inside to come almost even with Al, Jr. Almost. Al, Jr. won by .043 of a second. It was the closest finish ever at the Indy 500 and one that the Goodyear clan must replay ad nauseum.
>
> The Unser family holds a particular fondness for the Indy 500. Al, Jr.'s dad, Al Unser, Sr., won the race four times. Uncle Bobby Unser won three times. And Al, Jr. clocked in with his own win . . . by a heartbeat . . . in 1992.

that is oval-shaped (actually a triangular-shaped oval, as pictured on page 38). In addition, the track has a road course, which winds through part of the infield area. This allows the track to be used for different types of races. The 2.5-mile oval part of the track, for example, is used for stock car races such as the Daytona 500. The 3.56-mile combined oval and road course is used for sports car endurance races, such as the Rolex 24 at Daytona (originally called the 24 Hours of Daytona before expensive watches got into the act). In addition to auto racing, the Daytona International Speedway is home to a number of other premier races, including the American Motorcycle Association Superbike Classic and Motorcycle Races Championship Cup Series.

Some describe the experience of the Daytona 500 as the "largest picnic in the world." Two days after the race is over, the race for the following year is sold out. This is passion, ladies. Picture 150,000 people driving to this big tri-oval track in northern Florida on U.S. 92 in every type of vehicle imaginable—RVs, motorhomes, cars, trucks, vans, and mini-buses. Once the crowds arrive—and many come seven to ten days before the big race just to catch the pre-race fever—the first vehicles park in lots located within the infield area of the huge track, then the parking lots outside the track fill up.

The Daytona International Speedway has to be seen to be appreciated. Remember the first time you walked into a professional baseball stadium? Remember the brilliance of the bright green grass of the playing field, the smell of the tantalizing hot dogs, and the exciting buzz of the crowd? It is the same with Daytona. I can tell you that the track is two-and-a-half miles around, but you can't imagine just how massive this is until you actually see it. As you near the track from U.S. 92, the stands appear to grow. After all, it does fit 150,000 people.

Remember, when you arrive at Daytona, you are entering more than a speedway—it's more like a small country. We're talking 480 acres of stands, racetrack, picnic areas, and the recently opened Daytona USA. This entertainment complex details the history of motorsports in the Daytona Beach area in a fun, interactive way. This speedway is a tourist attraction. And, like the Indianapolis Motor Speedway, it is really more than a track—it's an event unto itself.

Ontario Motor Speedway

The Ontario Motor Speedway, which is not in Ontario, Canada, but forty miles from Los Angeles (Don't ask. I just don't have all the answers), is a facsimile of the Indianapolis racetrack, but better. The Indy oval is flat on the ground; spectators can see the cars only as they zoom by. The back side of Ontario's track is elevated thirty feet higher than in the front, making the entire race visible to those in the grandstands and bleachers. This speedway's garage area is an attraction in itself and open for public viewing. It has other things too, but again, let's not burden ourselves with too many facts. Less is more.

Other Superspeedways

As mentioned in Chapter 3, Indy cars race on superspeedways, temporary road courses, and permanent road courses. All superspeedways are at least one mile long and are considered the "big-time" tracks. In addition to the tracks at Daytona and Indianapolis, other famous superspeedways are Charlotte Motor Speedway, Michigan International Speedway, Darlington International Speedway, Atlanta International Speedway, and Dover Downs International Speedway

Auto Racing Tracks

The tracks below are just a sampling of those found in the United States. Note how they differ in shapes and lengths.

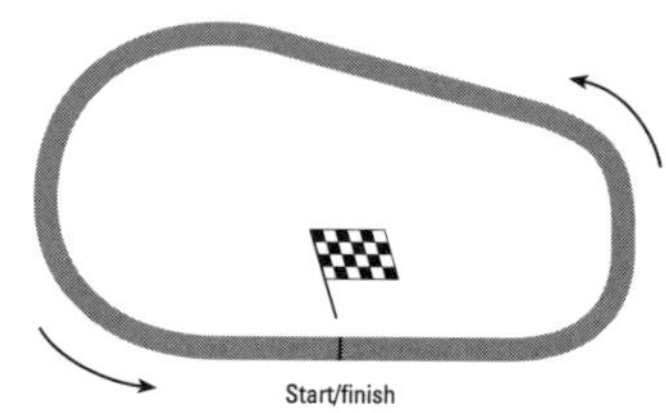

Darlington Raceway, Darlington, SC
Egg-Shaped Oval Course; 1.366 miles.

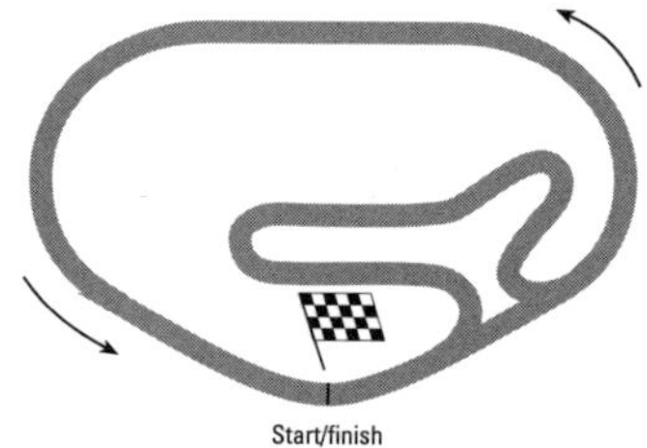

Daytona International Speedway, Daytona Beach, FL
Tri-Oval Course; 2.5 miles. Also includes a road course within the interior area of the track.

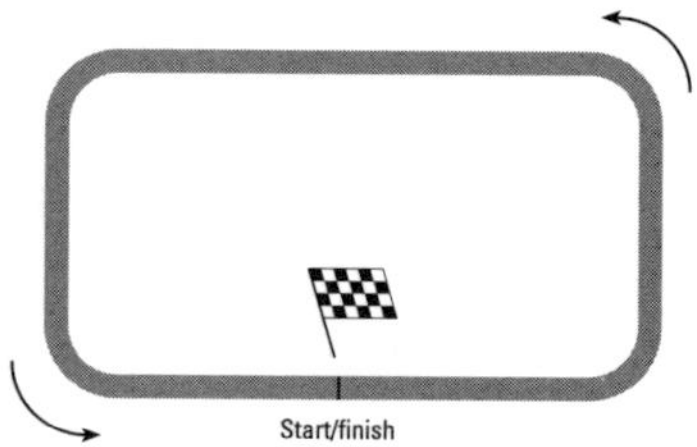

Indianapolis Motor Speedway, Indianapolis, IN
Oval Course; 2.5 miles.

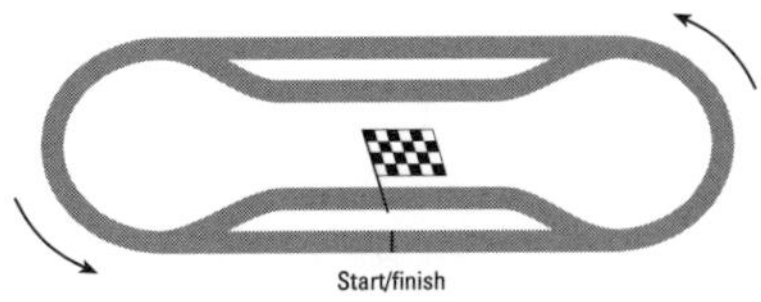

Martinsville Speedway, Martinsville, VA
Elongated Oval Course; 0.526 miles.

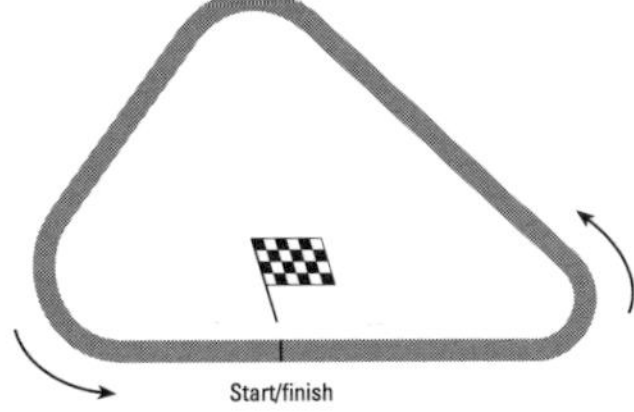

Pocono International Raceway, Long Pond, PA
Triangular Oval Course; 2.5 miles.

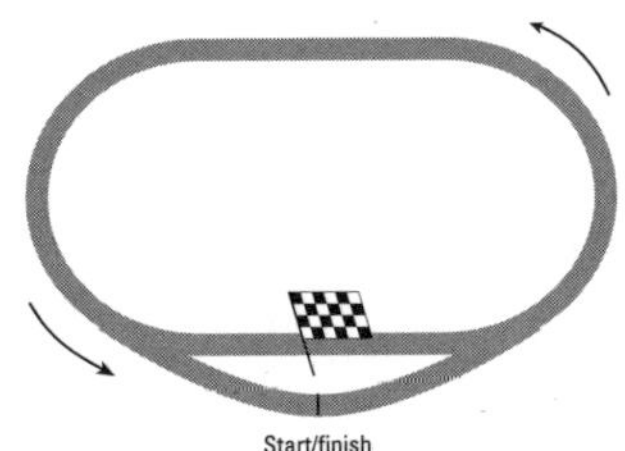

Talladega Superspeedway, Talladega, AL
Tri-Oval Course; 2.66 miles.

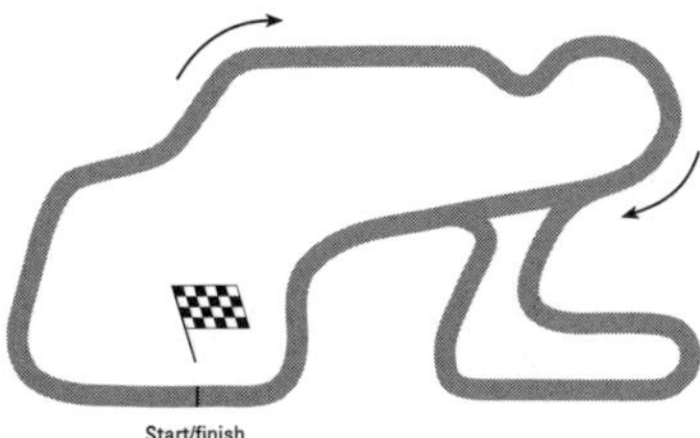

Watkins Glen International, Watkins Glen, NY
Permanent Road Course; 2.45 miles.

in Delaware. Superspeedways run longer races—in the hundreds of miles—for large cash prizes. As you would imagine, the longer the race, the bigger the purse. More miles, more money.

Grand Prix Tracks

Often, Formula One Grand Prix races are run on roads, many of which are tortuous. The Grand Prix course in Holland, for example, winds every which way but up along grassy sand dunes with whipping cold winds off the North Sea. In Monaco, the Grand Prix is run on extremely narrow streets that dip and then rise constantly. The original road course in Nurburgring, Germany, which has been redesigned for safety purposes, was considered one of the most difficult and dangerous of all Grand Prix tracks. Called The Ring, it was more like The Hell on Wheels. The track was 14-miles of roadways with 170 sharp curves and bends that ran through mountainous and heavily forested rural terrain. This race was often plagued by rain, which caused cars to become airborne as they hit peaks at high speed. All this and no stewardess. No thank you.

In the United States, one of the most famous Grand Prix races—the Watkins Glen International or "The Glen"—takes place in the village of Watkins Glen, located in the Finger Lakes region of New York State. In 1948, sports cars raced on a 6.6-mile course through the streets of Watkins Glen. It was the first post-World War II road race in the United States. Racing fever gripped those upstate New Yorkers and a

Road Rage!

On September 15, 1986, racer Jack Ingram was fined $5,000 and received a two-week suspension . . . and he should have considered himself lucky. These punishments were the result of his behavior during a race at the new Asheville Speedway. Here's what happened.

Jack was vying for the lead when his car got too close to some of the others and was bumped off the track. This did not make Jack happy. In fact, he went ballistic. He proceeded to turn his car around and drive back onto the speedway. This in itself is not horrible until you realize that Jack chose to drive back onto the speedway in the opposite direction of the other cars. He drove directly and purposely into one of his competitors, broadsiding him and causing massive chaos at the same time. Jack's name was found on very few Christmas card lists that year.

permanent 2.3-mile track was built in 1956. Five years later, Formula One stars came to the Glen for the Watkins Glen Grand Prix. The Glen soon became the site of many types of racing, including NASCAR and CART Indy car racing. In 1981, the track closed due to financial challenges, but it was bought in 1983 by the International Speedway Corporation and Corning (as in glass) Enterprises and reopened in 1984. The Glen is back in a big way, hosting New York's largest motorsports event—the NASCAR Winston Cup Series' Bud at the Glen. The Zippo (as in lighter) U.S. Vintage Grand Prix is also held here. They even re-enact the original 6.6-mile race through the town itself, which draws spectators from around the world.

As diverse as the cars are in the sport of auto racing, so are the tracks. Many tracks are located in communities that are not hubs of the world. In places like Bridgehampton, New York; Louden, New Hampshire; Elkhart Lake, Wisconsin; and Lime Rock, Connecticut, the tracks *are* the towns. What's Daytona without the Speedway or Indianapolis, too, for that matter? These tracks define many of the communities in which they are situated. They draw tourists that fill the coffers of the local hotels, restaurants, and stores. For those of you who thought auto racing tracks were just a bunch of dirt or a strip of pavement, now you know better.

Okay, let's take a moment to recap. We've met the cars and introduced ourselves to the tracks. Next, let's find out who runs this crazy sport called auto racing. For this you will need lots of paper, a number-two lead pencil with an eraser, and a big pot of coffee. Good luck.

Hellooooo . . .
Who's In Charge Here?

Every sport has some sort of governing body that makes the rules, oversees all that goes on, and serves as the final word when needed. Most sports have a board of directors and a commissioner or head honcho. Not so in auto racing. In auto racing, there are many sanctioning bodies that govern or authorize a variety of different races. Drivers are licensed by a particular sanctioning body and belong to different leagues. They race only in the events that are sanctioned by that league. Have you ever seen the word "sanctioned" used this much in your entire life? Have you ever seen the word "sanction" used period?

The whole sanctioning body business started in 1904. It was then that the American Automobile Association (AAA. Yes, the wonderful people that jump your car's dead battery.) began authorizing major U.S. auto races and did so until 1955. In 1955, the United States Auto Club (USAC) was formed and became a real player. It ran the Indy 500 and all Indy car races. But things got messy in the 1970s when Indy car owners stepped away from the USAC and formed their own organization called the Championship Auto Racing Teams (CART) and held their own racing series. Then in the mid 1990s, CART split and another new league was born—the Indy Racing League (IRL). Are your eyes starting to blur? Your mouth getting dry?

It goes without saying that not all the sanctioning bodies like each other and there is feuding, in-fighting, and backbiting. Basically, it's, "My sanctioning body is better than your sanctioning body." It has to be one of the most confusing, competitive set-ups in all of sports. We're going to take a look at the organizations that sanction (there's that word again) major auto racing events. Let's try to make sense of it. Have a bottle of aspirin at the ready.

National Association for Stock Car Auto Racing (NASCAR)

Established in 1947, NASCAR is the top banana. Its drivers include Jeff Gordon, Mark Martin, Dale Earnhardt, and other big racing names. This is the governing body of the Winston Cup Series, the series that offers the greatest prize money. Races in the Winston Cup Series include the Daytona 500, the Darlington 400, the Las Vegas 400, the Coca Cola 600, the Brickyard 400, and many, many others—thirty-six races in all that take place from February through November. Nearly all of the races are run on oval tracks. Basically, any time you tune in a NASCAR race on television it will look the same. Lots of blurs going round and round and lots of loud car noise. At least now you know that those blurs are auto racing's cream of the crop.

The top driver, Jeff Gordon, made well over $6 million in both 1997 and 1998. But, cry not for the number ten driver, who, for example, in 1997 was Ernie Irvan. That year, he earned a lowly $1.6 million. May we all someday do as poorly as Ernie.

NASCAR has done a phenomenal job of establishing itself as the dominant entity in American motor sports. With great marketing, appealing personalities, and an event that's easy to follow, NASCAR can do no wrong.

The Federation Internationale De L'Automobile (FIA)

Formed back in 1904 in Paris, France, FIA is the governing body of Formula One races and considered the foremost authority on international racing. The most famous Formula One races are the Grand Prix races, and drivers compete in this arena for the title of World Driving Champion. Pretty impressive title, oui?

Formula One is the most popular form of auto racing in the world (not counting the United States). Formula One racers include people you probably have never heard of, like Mika Hakkinen, Jacques

Villeneuve, and Michael Schumacher (See? Told you!). The races are held worldwide in places like France, Spain, Brazil, and Australia.

FIA is considered a big mucky muck in the motor sports world. Don't mess with them or they'll sanction you, too.

National Hot Rod Association (NHRA)

The NHRA governs drag racing and, with close to 85,000 members, is the largest motorsports organization in the world. Founded in 1951, it's goal was to establish drag racing rules and safety guidelines. Just as NASCAR runs its Winston Cup Series, the NHRA runs its Winston Drag Racing Series, which includes some twenty events. Drivers earn points on how they finish in each race, and the one with the most points at the end is named NHRA Season Champion. Close to 2 million people attend NHRA events every year. The NHRA also runs a Junior Drag Racing League for young dragsters yearning to be old dragsters.

Championship Auto Racing Team (CART) and Indy Racing League (IRL)

Now we get into murky waters. CART is the sanctioning body that was born in 1978 by Indy car owners who were not happy with the United States Auto

Club (USAC) leadership. Actually, it was a money thing. The owners (the ones who own the cars, get the sponsors, and hire the drivers) weren't making enough, so they decided to take things into their own hands. CART replaced USAC's reign in the world of Indy car racing. Everything was hunky dory for a time, but in the mid 1990s, some CART owners were unhappy and left CART to form a new league—the Indy Racing League (IRL). The issues that broke CART apart are difficult to understand for anyone who is not in the business itself. Just trust me when I say that these guys simply weren't happy, so they left the party.

The founder of the IRL is also the president of the Indianapolis Motor Speedway, so, as you can guess, the Indy 500 is now an IRL-sanctioned event, and none of the drivers licensed by CART are interested in participating. As a result of all this craziness, the Indy 500 has suffered. The race no longer has the great drivers competing together anymore—some drive for IRL and others drive for CART. Can you imagine the sport of baseball having a World Series that does not feature the best teams in the sport? Or one in which there are many World Series held at different stadiums at different times? This is what has happened to Indy car racing. And the numbers in the stands have greatly diminished. The Indianapolis 500, for example, which had attracted as many as 300,000 spectators in its heyday, is now attracting smaller crowds of closer to 100,000.

These two auto racing factions now carry on separately, but they do need to reconcile—the sport is hurting because of the breakup. Like a messy divorce, however, both sides are too far apart to make the necessary compromises to remarry. As a result, auto racing is a confusing mish-mash of leagues, championships,

Auto Racing 101

Auto racing has now joined the ranks of Baking 101 and Introduction to the Films of Woody Allen as a college "gut" course. At Appalachian State University in Boone, North Carolina, you can take "Southern Zoom—A History of Southern Stock Car Racing." A three-credit elective, "Southern Zoom" is taught by Mike Epley, a former auto racing writer. A recent Associated Press story quoted some students as saying, "This is a class they put here for me," "It's my destiny to take this class," and "The history of NASCAR? Where do I sign up?"

North Carolina, home of Jeff Gordon among others, is a virtual hotbed of motorsports education. Forsyth Technical in Winston-Salem offers an automotive degree with a concentration in race cars. Catawba Valley offers classes in the making of stock cars. And Rowan-Carrabus Community College in Salisbury awards a degree in motorsports management.

A PhD in NASCAR? What next?

prize money, sponsors . . . talk about needing a scorecard to know who's who. Don't even try. By the time you figure the whole thing out, it probably will have changed. And then, once it's changed, don't even try to figure out who's who and what's what, because, in time, it will change again. Confusing stuff.

So there you have it, the governing bodies. They make the rules, sanction the races, and oversee the leagues. In other words, they're the "big wheels" of auto racing.

6 Those Guys and Gals Who Go Really Fast for a Living

Probably the most interesting part of auto racing is the people. After all, tires, fenders, and engines are pretty darn dull. But the people behind the wheel make the sport interesting and generate the stories that excite the fans.

Famous Guys of Racing

Like a movie, the characters in auto racing fit a variety of roles. You have the good guys and the bad guys. You have the legends and the young up-and-comers. You have the leading man (or woman) and the supporting players. You have the big egos and the big mouths. And of course you have the heartthrobs. Let's start there! Where else?

Jeff Gordon

"Actually, I think wheelchairs are cool. If I was ever in one I'd have the fastest motorized wheelchair there was." This statement was uttered after NASCAR driver Jeff Gordon said that he did not fear death as much as being hurt and spending his life in a wheelchair. Eventually, however, he thought about what he said and changed his mind.

Let's begin with the important stuff, like Jeff Gordon's movie-star good looks. In his late twenties, Jeff stands 5 feet 7 inches tall, weighs 150 pounds, and has Tom Cruise-like good looks. This guy is every girl's summer dream. He wins lots and lots of races and sponsors love him. He's the face of auto racing, which is just what a sport filled with men wearing helmets needs.

Now let's move on to his auto racing accomplishments. In 1998, Gordon became the first driver of the modern era to record ten wins for three straight seasons. Since his first year in 1993, Gordon has won $22 million in prize money (this does not include the millions he earns in sponsorships).

Gordon is one of only four drivers in the history of auto racing to win three of NASCAR's top four events in one season, which translates into a $1-million bonus. He is the first driver to win two $1-million bonuses in one season. The other bonus, called "The No Bull 5" is given by Winston for winning two of the five races in the Winston Cup Series. In 1995, he was the youngest driver to win a NASCAR championship. Gordon is also the first driver ever to win the same superspeedway race—the Southern 500—four straight times. No one has won that race more than twice in the last forty-nine years. He has also won races on eighteen of the twenty-one current Winston Cup tracks.

If auto racing were rap, he'd be Puff Daddy. If it were books, he'd be Stephen King. If it were hit TV shows, this guy would be Buffy the Vampire Slayer! He defines the sport today, and because he is so young, one can only imagine that we will be seeing decades more of Jeff Gordon. Unless, of course he says, "Gee, I've earned like $300 million. Maybe I'll take a breather." Not bloody likely.

Mario Andretti

If you asked most people to name just one race car driver, there is no doubt that the name uttered most often would be "Mario Andretti." And there's good reason for that. This guy has been a winner in all types of auto racing, at all levels of competition, for close to four decades. When your father drove the car too fast (you know, like 30 miles per hour), your mother would, at that point, scream, "Who do you think you are? Mario Andretti?" When a name works its way into the everyday vernacular, we're talking a legend. Let's let Mario's numbers tell the bulk of his legendary story:

- Thirty-six years as a driver.
- $11,552,154 career Indy car earnings.

- The only driver to win the Daytona 500 (1967), the Indy 500 (1969), and the Formula One world title (1978).
- The only driver to be named "Driver of the Year" in three decades—1967, 1978, and 1984.
- The first driver to win Indy car races in four decades—the 60s, 70s, 80s, and 90s.
- Second most Indy car victories in history, with fifty-two wins.
- Winner of twelve Formula One races (in his spare time?).
- Competed against his son Michael, his son Jeff, and his nephew John in the 1991 IndyCar Series, marking the first time four family members had raced together in the same series. (He had time to make babies?)
- Enshrined in three Halls of Fame—the Indianapolis 500 Hall of Fame, the Motor Sports Hall of Fame, and the Sprint Car Hall of Fame.

Mario may have had a rich life, but it sure didn't start that way. Born in 1940 in Italy, Mario's family lived in a refugee camp from the time he was eight years old until he reached fifteen. In 1955, the Andrettis finally received a United States visa and moved to Pennsylvania with $125 in their pockets. Triumphing over adversity, Mario began racing four years later and started winning. He won twenty races in his first two seasons, and the rest, as they say, is history.

Food for Thought

Mario Andretti once said, "If I stay home one weekend, I become irritable. I can't help it. But if there's a race in Timbuktu, I've got to be there. I want to keep driving for as long as I can. I figure I was put on this earth to drive race cars. I love race cars and that's why I get involved with so many different types of them. One of the great thrills of my life is being given a new race car that is very sophisticated and making it perform to the utmost of my capabilities. It's simple, really. I enjoy racing. I would give up everything—my home, my family, everything I've gained—to stay in racing."

And Mrs. Andretti replied, "Thanks honey, let me introduce you to the kitchen where you'll be making your own meals from now on."

From $125 to $11,000,000. Now, that's a return on one's investment! Eat your heart out, Donald Trump!

A.J. Foyt

The only driver with more Indy car victories (sixty-seven) than Mario Andretti, or anyone else for that matter, is A.J. Foyt. His nickname is "Supertex." Like

A.J. isn't catchy enough. A.J. grew up in Texas and made his career choice at age five. His dad ran a garage that specialized in race cars, and little A.J. was obviously bitten by the bug (and we ain't talking a VW bug). A.J. always liked fast cars and when he was eighteen, he become a popular fixture on the Midwestern midget racing circuit. But he didn't stop at those midgets, which, by the way, go as fast as 115 miles an hour. A.J. raced basically everything everywhere. He was proficient with the midgets, sprint cars, stock cars, sports cars, and Indy cars. He loved to drive and he didn't care what he drove.

A.J. Foyt proved his love for auto racing by winning lots of major races. He is the only driver to win the Indy 500, the Daytona 500, the 24 Hours of Daytona, and the 24 Hours of LeMans. He's the first driver to win the Indy 500 four times and the only driver to win the Indy car championship seven times. He was particularly good at Indy, qualifying for a record thirty-five Indy 500s in a row from age twenty-three to age fifty-seven. In 1987, he went very, very fast and set a world speed record by going 257 miles per hour.

Now, take some guesses as to what the A.J. stands for (and yes, the answer is upside down on top of page 57, but must you cheat so soon?)

1. Apple Juice Foyt
2. Apricot Jam Foyt
3. Anaconda in the Jungle Foyt
4. Acrid Jockstrap Foyt
5. All of the Jabove

Answer: Anthony Joseph

Richard Petty

. . . 6 foot 2, eyes of blue . . . Actually very few people ever see the color of Richard Petty's eyes because of his trademark big, black Ray Charles sunglasses. But, really, what's the importance of eye color when you've won more stock car races than anyone in history, and your total career winnings are comfortably over $7,000,000? These are just the beginning of the accomplishments of Richard Petty, a man understandably called "The King" or "King Richard."

Son of NASCAR legend Lee Petty (Lee won the first Daytona 500), Richard did his daddy proud, winning a phenomenal seven NASCAR Winston Cup championships in 1964, 1967, 1971, 1972, 1974, 1975, and 1979. He also set a record in 1967 by winning twenty-seven races in one season, ten of them in a row!

Over his thirty-five year career, Richard Petty won 200 races and finished in the top ten 700 times. His 200 victories were almost twice as many as his closest competitor. He was the first stock car racer to pass $1 million in career earnings, and he won six-figure prize money an impressive twenty-four times. He also managed to have four kids. His only son, Kyle, is now a top racer as well. Good genes abound in that Petty family. Watch out for the grandkids!

Dale Earnhardt

When Dale Earnhardt beat the Susan Lucci curse in 1998, he said, "I've got that goddamn monkey off my back!" One of the greatest stock car racers in history, and considered the best NASCAR racer of his generation, Dale was stymied by the Daytona 500 to the tune of zero wins in nineteen attempts. He just could not win it. He'd often dominate the race, but never finish first. In an excruciating 1990 Daytona, for instance, he led for 499 miles before shredding a tire on the final lap. But, in 1998, in the fiftieth anniversary year of NASCAR and on his twentieth try, mercury came out of retrograde and Dale Earnhardt won the Daytona 500!

Dale is the top NASCAR all-time money winner with an astounding $32,707,585. He's been the Winston Cup NASCAR Champion seven times—in 1980, 1986, 1987, 1990, 1991, 1993, and 1994—tying him with Richard Petty. He was the 1979 Rookie of the Year, and when he followed that with his 1980 Championship, he became the first driver to win both awards in consecutive years.

Earnhardt seems to like the dramatic. When he won the elusive Daytona 500, he pulled out a stuffed monkey, signifying the monkey that had been on his back for nineteen years, and threw it at the crowd of reporters. Most of those reporters had probably arrived at Daytona wondering how Dale was going to lose the race this time. He then boldly announced that he would go on to win his eighth NASCAR championship in 1998, which would break the record he and Petty held. Didn't happen. But Earnhardt was a Daytona bridesmaid no more, and that had to feel awfully good.

The Gals of Auto Racing

"Auto racing is genderless. The car doesn't know the difference," said racer Lyn St. James. It should come as no surprise that women too are capable of sitting in a car and driving around and around really fast. And, should we get lost . . . we ask for directions!

As easy as driving a car sounds, you won't need more than two hands to count the number of women who have successfully broken through the glass ceiling of auto racing. It's one thing to become a successful female tennis player, figure skater, marathoner, golfer, or any of the sports that embrace the female athlete. Auto racing is another story. If ever the "good ol' boy" network reigned supreme, it's in this male-dominated sport. There are, however, a number of women who have beaten the odds in auto racing. They have an "I can do anything" attitude that we all wish we could bottle and save for future use. Let's take a look at three of these women and note their accomplishments.

Janet Guthrie

"I drive the car. I don't carry it," is Janet Guthrie's standard response when asked whether a woman can compete with men in auto racing.

In 1977, Janet became the first woman to race in the Indianapolis 500. In that same year, she was named Top Rookie at the Daytona 500. One year earlier, she was the first woman to compete in a NASCAR Winston Cup superspeedway stock car race. And she was pretty good, too. She finished ninth in the Indy 500 in 1978.

Guthrie had always been attracted to things that went fast. Before taking on auto racing she was a pilot, a flight instructor, and an aerospace engineer. She spent thirteen years on the auto racing circuit before being invited to Indy. Her helmet and driver's outfit are on display in the Smithsonian Institute, and she was one of the first women named to the Women's Sports Hall of Fame.

Lyn St. James

"My mom raised me to be well educated and refined. She felt the piano would help me learn to be a lady and give me something I could always fall back on. Racecar driving was not what she had in mind!"

Fifteen years after Janet Guthrie became the first woman to race the Indy 500, Lyn St. James became the second. Finishing eleventh in that race in 1992, St. James impressed many with her skill and competitive speed, and was named the prestigious Indy's "Rookie of the Year." She was the first female ever to receive this honor, and what's even more impressive is that St. James was in her forties at the time. She finished first at Watkins Glen, New York, in 1985, becoming the first woman ever to win a solo North American

I've Heard of Seat Belts, But This Is Ridiculous . . .

Driver Buddy Baker crashed into a wall at the Smokey Mountain Raceway on June 6, 1968. An ambulance was summoned immediately. The emergency crew strapped Buddy to a gurney and the ambulance rushed off to the hospital. But those wacky guys forgot to close and lock the back doors of the ambulance. As the ambulance burned rubber off the track, yep, you guessed it, the doors opened and the gurney flew out with ole Buddy strapped on and helpless. Gurney and Buddy rolled across the track before thousands of shocked spectators and dozens of flabbergasted auto racers. Cars steered all around Buddy on gurney with some just narrowly missing him. But miss him they did, and Buddy went on to become a major player on the NASCAR circuit for another twenty years.

professional road race of any kind. In 1985, she also became the first woman to average more than 200 miles per hour on an oval track.

A pioneer on other fronts as well, in 1995, St. James was the first woman to be in the announcers booth for auto racing. She also holds the women's closed-course speed record at a blistering 225 miles per hour.

Auto racer, television commentator, wife, mother, spokesperson . . . St. James founded the Lyn St. James Foundation in 1993. This foundation focuses on activities and programs for automotive safety and driver development, especially for aspiring female racecar drivers. She also runs the Lynn St. James Motor Sports driving school in Daytona Beach, Florida, for women only. If you want to go really fast for a living, give them a call.

Shirley Muldowney

"I always knew this wouldn't be an easy profession. But the attitudes against me didn't bother me. Trying to hold onto a 1,700-pound car with a 2,000-horsepower engine is hard work, and anyone that says different is out of his mind."

The first woman to be licensed by the National Hot Rod Association (NHRA), Shirley Muldowney was the first driver, male or female, to repeat as NHRA Winston World Champion. She was the first driver to win that championship three times, in 1977, 1980, and 1982. The movie *Heart Like a Wheel*, starring Bonnie Bedelia, chronicled Shirley's career.

Shirley drives dragsters, and this has nothing to do with a particular way of dressing. Drag racing is a true mano-a-mano sport and Shirley introduced the new concept of woman-a-mano. She was accepted because she was so damn good. Shirley was the first woman to be inducted into the Motorsports Hall of Fame and was named to the American Auto Racing Writer and Broadcasters Association All American Team five times. In 1997, Shirley set the International Hot Rod Association's (yes, the IHRA) national speed record by clocking in at 294.98 miles per hour.

THE PITS

You've heard of making a pit stop . . . taking a break from the action, a moment for a non-fat latte in a busy day. Well, this term originates from the world of auto racing, where, along the track, there's an area called the pits. This is where drivers stop during the race to fill up with gas, make any necessary repairs, and check the overall condition of their cars. The pit crew is the group of people in the pits who can change four tires and refuel a car in the time it takes most of us to get out of bed. Every second counts, particularly when you realize that some races are won by less than a second.

It works like this. Before the race, the car is in a garage, which often is like a paddock or parking lot. Once the car is unloaded from a trailer or truck, the mechanics snap into action and get the car ready for competition. When it comes to the big-car classes like NASCAR, getting the car in perfect shape for the race is the responsibility of the crew chief. He oversees everything, both in the garage and often in the pits as well. The crew chief is paid a salary and a percentage of the winnings. This can be a lot of cash when you realize that many of these drivers earn well over a million dollars a year. For those of us who think a lug nut comes in a Planter's bottle, a career as a crew chief would be rather unrealistic.

In the wee hours before a big race, it is amazing to see the work that still needs to be done. There are cars without engines, cars without wheels, cars with wheels but no doors. Not to worry. These mechanics work fast and they're well choreographed. Watching them work is like watching a greasy ballet!

Before you know it, the cars are ready. The crew chief fires up the engine and calls for the driver. A thorough check of all safety equipment follows, and the driver's fire-resistant suit is carefully inspected—same for his crash helmet and face shield. Cracks, holes, or any imperfections can spell disaster. A fire extinguisher, many of which operate automatically via a heat-sensing device, is placed in the car.

Once the race begins, the job of keeping that car humming is the responsibility of the pit crew. A pit crew practices daily to perfect its necessary duties of refueling, changing tires, wiping windshields, and blending a nice piña colada. As with the driver, the pit crew's goal is to be very fast. They have only seconds in which to work.

Each driver wears a headset that keeps him in constant contact with his or her pit crew throughout the race. The crew will tell the driver when the tires are wearing down or fuel is low, or it may alert the driver as to the number of laps that are left. And sometimes it will tell him that Tommy Lee and Pamela Anderson have broken up again. Obviously, they tell him only the important stuff.

When the pit crew instructs a driver to come in for a pit stop, he rarely argues. Trying not to lose a moment of time, he usually brakes late and swerves into the pit area at the last moment. The crew is ready. Before the car comes to a full stop, they're already holding tires, jacks, and other who-knows-what-they-are car stuff like nozzles, wire, and tubing. The fuelers start fueling, the tiremen start tiring, the jackmen are jacking, and the butcher, the baker, and the candlestick maker are doing what they do best as well. There isn't a second to spare—17, 18, 19 seconds can translate into 17,000, 18,000, 19,000 fewer dollars in prize money.

Then, the fuelers uncouple their hoses, the jackman lowers the new wheel onto the pavement, and the crew chief whacks the driver on the helmet signaling, "Go!" And back to the race he goes, all spiffed up and perfect again.

The pit crew is living proof that the driver may be king, but, as in most professions, it's all the king's men that keep him on top.

Other Women Drivers

There are a number of other women of racing. There's Cleo Chandler, the great-grandmother drag racer who started her driving career at age sixty-eight! Others include Linda "First Lady of Auto Racing" Vaughn, Alice Ridpath, Maureen Kempston Darkes, and current-day hot rod top dog Amy Faulk. Household names, none. Pioneers, most. Kick-ass, take-no-prisoners women with cojones, all.

There you have it—some of those people who drive the cars in the races on the tracks. We've learned that there are men as well as women who can drive faster than one can fathom, in cars as diverse as one can imagine, in a variety of races, on tracks that range from short and gravelly to long and paved.

We've also learned that this auto racing thing is not as simple as we thought it was. It's far from "man in a car goes very fast in a circle." But this learning thing isn't over yet. Here comes the glossary—terms that you can mix and match to impress your friends. Burn rubber to the next chapter.

Terms That'll Make You Sound Like You Know What You're Talkin' About

Auto racing, like all sports, has its very own special language and symbols. It's important to know some, not all, of the unique terms that make up and define a sport so that you can mingle with the devotees.

Key Terms

What follows are some of the basic terms of auto racing. They will help you get by in a roomful of auto racing aficionados.

Bent Eight. Sounds kinky, but a bent eight is simply a V-8 engine. This is not an engine that runs on V8 juice instead of gasoline, although wouldn't that be nutritious? This is an engine with eight cylinders. Most cars have four, some have six, and only the really powerful have eight.

Boogered Up. An undeniably appealing term with wonderful visual imagery that basically means things did not go as planned, or . . . you messed up and your car crashed.

Cockpit. This is where the driver sits. Sometimes a cockpit is open, like on the cars in those Grand Prix races. Kinda like a convertible with the top down.

Crew Chief. This is the guy in charge of keeping the race car in top shape. These days, he's more of the delegator or brains behind the operation and rarely gets his hands dirty. He's like the director of a play, and all of the mechanics are his actors.

Fuel Cell. The car's fuel is kept in this rubbery object that looks a lot like an old-fashioned hot water bottle. Inside the fuel cell is a spongy material that soaks up any fuel that might leak out after a crash. This helps prevent fires, a very real risk in the world of auto racing.

Groove. This the best and shortest line around a race course. When one is "in the groove," all is right with the world. When one is "groovy" one is old and embarrassing to one's children.

Happy Hour. It's not what you think, although we can safely assume there's plenty of that after the race. Happy hour is the last official practice before a race.

Head Wrench. Crew chief. No relation to Head Pliers.

Lugs. These are the five nuts that keep the wheel on the axle. It's also what the Head Wrench calls his Lesser Wrenches, as in, "Come here, you buncha lugs."

Modified. Sometimes you'll hear about so-and-so driving a "Ford modified car." This means a car with a closed cockpit but open wheels. What's an open wheel, you ask? A wheel that is not closed. Okay? All right, all right. It means no fenders.

Pole Position. Considered the prime spot in the race, the pole position is awarded to the driver with the fastest qualifying time. It is the inside position of the front row at the start of the race and in no way means that that driver will win the race. In fact, out of the eighty-two Indy 500s that have been run between 1911 and 1998 (there were no races in 1917, 1918, 1942, 1943, 1944, or 1945), only sixteen were won by drivers who had the pole position. That's about 20 percent, which means 80 percent of the winners were stuck elsewhere and won despite the odds.

Roll Cage. Hollow steel tubing that is welded together to form a protective cage around the driver of stock cars. In the event of an accident, the roll cage prevents the driver from becoming airborne or from being crushed. Roll cages are one reason drivers are often able to walk away after a horrific crash.

Rubber. The tires. Burn 'em baby!

Sanctioned Race. This is an official race according to the governing body of the sport. Of course, since no one really knows who the governing body of the sport is these days, give me a call and I'll be happy to sanction your race.

Splash 'n Go. This is not a cologne thing. It means a racer makes a quick pit stop just for refueling and nothing more.

Stop 'n Go Penalty. If a racer goes too fast in the pits or drives without regard to safety, such as in reverse, he will be given a stop 'n go penalty. The driver must bring his or her car onto pit road, which is the road where the pit crews work, and wait one full second before starting again. Geez, what happens if you purposely hit someone? Two full seconds?

Tachometer. Stock cars, the kind of cars that Jeff Gordon and other NASCAR racers drive, do not have speedometers, they have tachometers. They also, by the way, do not have upholstery, brake lights, or any seats besides the driver's, but that has nothing to do with defining the tachometer. Just thought it was an interesting tidbit of knowledge. The tachometer measures how hard the engine is working as opposed to how fast the car is going. It measures the engine's revolutions per minute or RPMs, and lets the driver know when to shift gears.

Trading Paint. This is a cuddly phrase for a rather unseemly situation. It's used when one car gently nudges another car so that their respective paints meet each other.

Window Net. This is a strong piece of nylon webbing that hangs across the driver's side window. Not only does it keep the driver's head and arms from flying out during an accident, it also serves as a shield, preventing debris from entering the cockpit and injuring the driver.

Wrench. A mechanic. Often married to a wench, sometimes having quite a stench, and, if Jewish, might be called a mensch.

The Flags

You cannot communicate easily with drivers who are racing at 200 miles per hour. Yelling, "Hey you, slow down," will not have much impact as they whiz by in a blur. This is why auto racing has colored flags to visually communicate to the drivers. Like stoplights, these flags are an international, universal method of communication. The following is a listing of these flags and what they stand for.

Green Flag. The race has begun. When the green flag is waved by the race official it's time to press that gas pedal. For many of us, the green flag is like the yellow on a traffic light. Go!

Yellow Flag. Caution. The yellow flag can indicate an accident, oil slick, or other upcoming potential

THOSE CRAZY ACRONYMS (TCA)

Never has there been a sport so filled with hard-to-understand acronyms as auto racing. Basketball has the NBA (National Basketball Association) and the WNBA (Women's National Basketball Association). It used to have the ABA (American Basketball Association) and the ABL (American Basketball League), but that was six letters too many and both of these leagues are gone. Baseball has the AL (American League) and the NL (National League), and both leagues are a part of MLB (Major League Baseball). Pretty simple. All sports have international leagues and minor leagues or college leagues, but none come close to the number of different leagues, circuits, or associations that auto racing has. Let's take a look at some of Those Crazy Acronyms (TCA) and see what they stand for.

hazard. When the yellow flag is unfurled, there is no passing allowed. Bobby Unser learned this the hard way in a bizarre set of events surrounding the 1981 Indy 500. Unser's car had finished first, but he was penalized one lap for passing other cars under a yellow caution flag. The victory was given instead to second-place finisher Mario Andretti. Unser appealed the

NASCAR.	National Association of Stock Car Auto Racing
NHRA.	National Hot Rod Association
IHRA.	International Hot Rod Association
CART.	Championship Auto Racing Teams
IRL.	Indy Racing League
IMSA.	International Motor Sports Association
USAC.	United States Auto Club
SCCA.	Sports Car Club of America

And this is just the tip of the iceberg! There's the FSAE, ARCA, CASCAR, IROC, and more! Why, I ask you? Why can't we just all get along and belong to the AARA, the American Auto Racing Association, which I just created and hope will soon catch on and save us all the time and trouble of learning TCAs.

decision and a panel ruled the penalty was in fact too severe. They fined Unser $40,000 but restored the victory to him. Quite the sport, no?

Red Flag. You guessed it . . . STOP! At once! No pussy-footing around by slowing to a stop. Drivers must come to an immediate halt.

Black Flag. Time for a pit stop. The driver must head to the pits for refueling, repairs, or other needs. As opposed to many of us who stop along the way during a long trip, a pit stop is not the time for a nosh and reapplication of makeup.

Black-and-White Checkered Flag. You won! Go to Disneyland!

There you have it. Some bon mots to toss about. Try them in a sentence, like "I never saw a car go so fast. The tachometer must have been off the chart," or "Did you hear the one about the Russian, the Czech, and the Pole position?"

Meet the Martins An "Auto" Biography

When I first met Mark I knew little, almost nothing, about auto racing. It wasn't something I grew up with as a kid, it wasn't something my parents were passionate about, it just wasn't a part of my life. Obviously, things have changed. But, I did want to say to all of you women out there, don't despair . . . you can learn about auto racing, and you can learn to love it. If I did, you can.

A lot of people are interested in how Mark and I got together and what the life of an auto racing family is like. Happy to oblige. Here's a bit about us.

Mark and I met in 1983 through his sister when we both lived in Arkansas. It didn't take long before I knew that he was "the one." Six months to be exact. For many women, it takes longer to find the perfect dress! For me, it was obvious pretty quickly that I'd found the perfect match. Within the year, we married in Memphis, Tennessee, and shortly thereafter we moved to Charlotte, North Carolina, where Mark had a home.

TOP RACING AND AUTO-RELATED MOVIES OF ALL TIME

How many times have you walked into your local video store committed to finding a great auto racing movie to watch on a rainy day? Never? That, my friend, is about to change. Herewith are the nominees for the "nonexistent" auto racing film festival. Spring for the three dollars and bring one home. Settle back on the couch, dab a little motor oil behind your ears, and get ready for the v-r-o-o-o-movies.

Days of Thunder. Tom Cruise. Yum. Nuff said.

Heart Like a Wheel. Stars Bonnie Bedelia as hot rodder Shirley Muldowney—the first woman inducted into the Motorsports Hall of Fame. Her story is an inspiration for all women.

American Graffiti. A salute to the 1960s, which was a big car era (what with drive-in movies and drive-up hamburger joints). There's a great drag race in the film, as well.

Rebel Without a Cause. Has a harrowing drag race with devastating results. The good news is the film stars James Dean and Sal Mineo. Yum. Yum.

Ben Hur. Hey, those chariots had wheels.

Breaking Away. Hey, those bikes had wheels.

The French Connection. Includes a car chase that takes your breath away.

Grand Prix. A classic 1966 auto race-focused drama with a stellar cast including James Garner and Eva Marie Saint.

Bullitt. Has a fantastic car chase through the streets of San Francisco. Anything with Steve McQueen just screams cars.

Le Mans. Starring, you guessed it . . . Steve McQueen.

Greased Lightning. Story of Wendell Scott, the first black auto racing champion. Stars Richard Pryor.

Six Pack. The "Gambler" goes auto racing.

Personal auto movie favorites and further proof that a simple mind is behind this book include:

Chitty, Chitty Bang, Bang. What's better than a flying car?

The Love Bug. Stars a VW bug with a mind of its own.

It's a Mad, Mad, Mad, Mad World. Loads of cars in every shape and size take part in a road race to find a hidden treasure. Lots of fun, this film features a who's who of "B" stars.

From Charlotte it was on to Milwaukee, Wisconsin. From Milwaukee we relocated to Greensboro, North Carolina. And from Greensboro we moved to our present home in Daytona Beach, Florida. We Martins have certainly done our share of packing!

The world of auto racing was a lot for me to understand at first. I, like most people who are new to the sport, didn't quite understand the attraction of a bunch of cars driving around in a circle for four hours. But every time I went to a race, I learned something new, and it didn't take long before I began to catch the fever. I remember at one of my first races, I was struck by the fact that the tires didn't have any treads—they were totally smooth. Mark explained afterwards that slick tires run better on asphalt. Who knew? Auto racing became a constant source of learning for me.

In the beginning of our marriage, as you can imagine, I went to every race. But I was the mother of four girls from a previous marriage, and the responsibilities of motherhood certainly impacted my ability to travel at whim. Once my daughters entered their teen years, the demands on me as a parent meant I had to stay home more. Plus, you don't think I'd leave four teenage girls at home without supervision, do you?! I wouldn't have had a house to come home to! The girls are grown now and living in different cities throughout the country, but Mark and I do not suffer from "empty nest syndrome." We still have our son, Matt, who is now seven years old and keeps me very busy. There was a moment there when I thought I was done with birthday parties and Halloween costumes, but then along came Matt! And, of course, we're thrilled to have him. Proud of his dad, Matt likes auto racing and is already racing quarter midgets! If Matt decides to pursue auto racing as a career, Mark and I would support and encourage him. But, we'll see. After all, he's only in first grade. Let's not rush him!

There are a lot of people out there who think of all sports as high paid athletes with groupies in tow. Auto racing just isn't that way. Most of the drivers are married and most of the wives come to the races. It's tough to fool around on your wife when she's standing next to you! Mark and I also started a kind of trend for the other drivers and their families. Ten years ago, we bought a motor home and started traveling to all the races that way, bringing the motor home to the track and staying in it after the race as well. Now, many of the drivers and their families do the same. So, while other sports have their athletes staying in expensive hotels without their families, we stay in our motor home together. We like it that way.

More and more women are certainly coming to the races. I've noticed over the years that the female fan base for auto racing is really growing. Lots of women in the stands—lots of wives, daughters, and sisters of drivers. As I said, auto racing is a true family sport. You can see it by the fans. It's just a great, healthy all-American day out.

The other wives and I have developed some nice friendships. In most sports, the wives all sit together in a special area watching the game. In auto racing, it's a little different. For one thing, we don't sit in the grandstands. We stay in a special area within the infield of the track that is set aside just for us. Our motor homes are there, and we are able to go back and forth, getting beverages, a bite to eat, or whatever else we may need.

Mark is doing so well in the sport and has so many outside demands from sponsors like Valvoline,

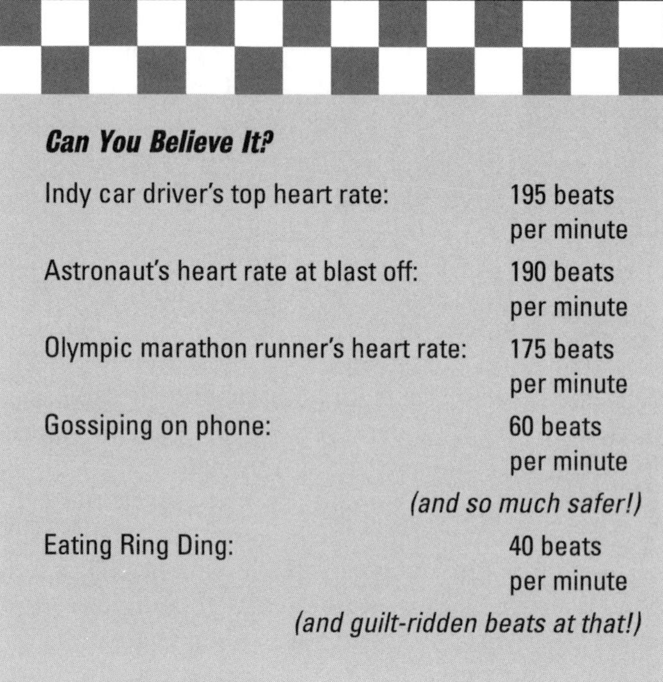

Can You Believe It?

Indy car driver's top heart rate:	195 beats per minute
Astronaut's heart rate at blast off:	190 beats per minute
Olympic marathon runner's heart rate:	175 beats per minute
Gossiping on phone:	60 beats per minute *(and so much safer!)*
Eating Ring Ding:	40 beats per minute *(and guilt-ridden beats at that!)*

Ford, and Winn Dixie, he's away from home a lot. Although he's racing ten months of the year, he is busy making appearances for his sponsors during the off-months of December and January. During these times, I do feel a bit like a single mom, but I'm not lonely. I keep very busy. Matt keeps me very busy. And following Mark's career keeps me very busy. It really is a good life.

But this auto racing life won't last forever. Inevitably, the time will come when Mark will hang up his helmet and call it a day. Luckily, he has quite a few other interests, so I don't believe I'll ever see him sitting around the living room growing fat with little to do. Recently he became a pilot, and I believe this interest will continue long after his auto racing career is over. Mark also inherited a portion of his dad's trucking business, which should also take a good deal of his time once he retires from driving as a career. So, we Martins will be busy. And that's just the way we like it!

Mark, Arlene, and Matt Martin

Bibliography

The Everything You Wanted to Know About Sports Encyclopedia. Neil Cohen, editor. New York: Bantam Books, 1994.

Golenbock, Peter. *American Zoom*. New York: MacMillan Publishing, 1993.

Radosta, John S. *The New York Times Complete Guide to Auto Racing*. Chicago: Quadrangle Books, 1971.

Wukovits, John F. *The Composite Guide to Auto Racing*. Philadelphia: Chelsea House Publishing, 1999.

Index